RAILWAYS OF THE R...
by Alon Siton

Published by Mainline & Maritime Ltd, 3 Broadleaze, Upper Seagry, near Chippenham, SN15 5EY
Tel: 01275 845012   www.mainlineandmaritime.co.uk   orders@mainlineandmaritime.co.uk
ISBN: 978-1-900340-79-3   Printed in the UK
All photographs from the Historical Railway Images Archive unless otherwise credited © Mainline & Maritime Ltd & Author 2020
All rights reserved. No part of this publication may be reproduced by any process without the prior written permission of the publisher.

Front Cover An Orenstein & Koppel 0-6-0T hauls a train up the Matheran Hill Railway.
Back Cover The Great Indian Peninsula Railway train carrying the Viceroy, Lord Curzon, enters Victoria Station in Bombay, on 30th April 1904, headed by 4-4-0 No. 63.
Above Bengal Nagpur Railway 4-6-2 No. 00104 (North British Locomotive Works, Glasgow 17822 / 1908).

Historical Background: The British Empire's Foray into India

It seems unimaginable today that the giant Indian subcontinent was once ruled by an island more than twenty times smaller its size and yet, Britain's hold of both India as well as the neighboring countries of Pakistan, Ceylon and Burma remains an historical fact. The conquest of what was popularly called "the jewel in the crown" had a deep effect on both nations, to the point that India alone became the most prominent of all of the British Empire's many colonies and dominions. By the middle of the 19th century, however, British rule was met with a wave of aggressive nationalism in southern Asia, triggering consecutive periods of relative stability and outbursts of violent dissent in protest of Britain's policy, especially in India. This went on until India was finally granted independence in 1947, no longer a crown colony but a free sovereign state.

The road to British presence in India was paved as early as 1600, under Queen Elizabeth I, who granted a Royal Charter to a group of British merchants wishing to explore the riches of southern Asia. Thus was created the East Indian Company (EIC). Interestingly, at first the company preferred to trade indirectly with India, and was instead focused on competing with the Dutch, the French and the Portuguese over control in the East Indies. When this failed, the EIC shifted its interests to India itself. In 1640, the company succeeded in securing a piece of land in southern India, and built a small fort named St. George, thereby signaling the start of the gradual British penetration into the rest of the country. The settlement that was formed around this region grew into the modern city of Madras (now called Chennai) with no fewer than seven million citizens.

Additional EIC forts and settlements sprang up all around India and the British were now leading traders in precious Indian goods, regularly exporting shipments of expensive spices to Europe. Before long, a private army was recruited from the local population and the EIC was involved in Indian politics. Simultaneously, the EIC was able to expand its presence in India by shipping in more men and materials than the other European powers. The local rulers, too, benefited handsomely from their dealings with the company, and tended to cooperate with Britain's intentions for India. By 1760, India was rapidly coming under direct British control, despite strong resistance from some of the Indian states that were not interested in doing business with the English. The opposition was crushed under the Duke of Wellington, who later defeated Napoleon in the famous battle of Waterloo. When the military campaign ended, the whole of India was subjugated to Britain and the foundations were laid for a new empire that was bigger than anything that the British had ever dreamt of.

By the mid-19th century, Indian nationalism was beginning to take form primarily because of the EIC's attitude towards the native Indians, with repeated demands for social and economic reforms. These strong anti-British sentiments resulted in the Indian Rebellion of 1857, which, although brutally suppressed, also led to the transfer of power from the East Indian Company to the British Government. The effect on the difficult living conditions in India was minor. The country's resources and the livelihood of its people were routinely exploited to fuel the industrial revolution in Britain, leading to a series of severe famines in India, even as late as 1943 in Bengal. The Indian economy was effectively ruined and millions of helpless native Indians perished from starvation, malaria and other deadly disease.

It was under these unpromising conditions that the British Raj in India officially began in 1857. The Raj (literally "rule" in Sanskrit) was also called Crown Rule in British India, including the Princely States which were ruled locally by indigenous princes or maharajas (under British control). At the head of the new Indian Empire was the British Monarch, in this case Queen Victoria who, in 1876, was declared Empress of India. The Raj ended formally in 1947, with the partition of the Indian Empire into two sovereign states - India and Pakistan, whose eastern part later became Bangladesh. Burma (today Myanmar) was administered as an autonomous province until 1937, when it became a separate colony, gaining its own independence from Britain in 1948. In numbers, the Raj consisted of eight main provinces under a British Commissioner or Governor, these being Assam, Bengal, Bombay, Burma, Central Provinces, Madras, Punjab and the United Provinces at the foot of the Himalaya Mountains. In 1900 alone, these territories had a total population of more than 200 million inhabitants in a combined area that was several times bigger than all of the UK.

The Beginning of Railways in India

Before going into more detail, it is worth mentioning that Britain's colonial presence in India remains a sensitive issue to this day. In the case of the railways, so goes the argument, the construction of the Indian railway system is often described as one of the ways in which Britain benefited the subcontinent, when in fact many other countries were perfectly capable of building their own railways without ever being colonized. Also, a railway system in India was originally the idea of the East India Company, specifically designed for the company's own purposes, that is, for the commercial, administrative and military control of the country. Finally, British shareholders are said to have made huge profits by investing in the new Indian railways companies, with guaranteed high returns that were paid entirely from Indian, and not British, taxes.

On top of that, there never was any real plan to build the railways for the comfort of the Indians themselves. Instead, the railways were built to carry Indian goods, such as coal, iron ore, cotton, spices and minerals, to be shipped off exclusively to British markets and factories. Passenger traffic took a lower priority, except when it served colonial interests, and the primitive third class compartments, with their hard wooden benches and no toilets, were positively unfit for human presence.

Racial segregation was another cause for constant frustration in India, as was the case elsewhere in the British Empire, particularly in Africa. Although "whites-only" compartments were cancelled for economic reasons, most Indians were barely able to afford third class travel, where the available space was often insufficient for their numbers and the conditions unacceptable. Another aspect was the prevailing view that the railways had to be staffed exclusively by Europeans to "protect the investment". This was especially true of signalmen, locomotive drivers and repair crews. The policy was maintained into the early 20th century with Europeans holding all the key positions, from executive members of the Railway Board to ticket collectors, and with salaries that were at European, not Indian, level.

Finally on this, it is argued that British economic interests took priority to Indian industrial efficiency. The railway workshops in Jamalpur (Bengal) and Ajmer (Rajputana) were established in 1862, and in 1878 their skillful Indian mechanics succeeded in designing and building their own steam locomotives. The British were alarmed at this, since the Indian-built locomotives were as good, and cheaper, than the British-made ones. In 1912, the British Government decided on a policy that made it impossible for Indian workshops to design and manufacture locomotives on a large scale, forcing the import into India of no fewer than 14,000 British locomotives, and another 3,000 from builders in Canada, the US and Germany. On the eve of independence, in 1947, India had lost the last surviving remnant of technical knowledge and had to seek Britain's assistance in setting up a locomotive factory in India. Ironically, the situation has changed dramatically since then and today, it is Britain that now relies extensively on Indian technical expertise.

India's railway history officially began with a pair of small industrial lines. The first one, in 1832, was The Red Hills Railway, which was part of a road-building project in Madras. The second line was built in 1845 to carry rocks for the construction of a new dam over the mighty Godavari River (India's second longest river after the Ganga).

Next to come was the creation of new Indian railway companies. On 8 May 1845, the Madras Railway Company was officially established, followed in the same year by the East Indian Railway. On 1 August 1849, the Great Indian Peninsula Railway was incorporated. To finance these large projects, the British Government offered an incentive in the form of a "guarantee system", providing free land and a lucrative 5% interest to any private British company that was willing to build railways and facilities in India. Work began shortly thereafter and India's first-ever passenger train departed Bombay's Bori Bunder station (later Victoria Terminus) to nearby Thane on 16 April 1853. Travelling the distance of 34 km in a little under one hour, the first train carried 400 passengers on a broad gauge (1,676 mm or 5 feet 6 inches) track. It was to be one of at least four official gauges used in India, ranging from broad to standard, meter and narrow gauge lines. The train was made of fourteen coaches and three 2-4-0 tender locomotives named "Sahib", "Sindh" and "Sultan" from a fleet of eight locomotives that were ordered new from Vulcan Foundry in 1852. Sadly, Sahib and Sultan appear to have been scrapped, but Sindh was spotted outside the GIPR Chief Mechanical Engineer's office in Bombay until 1953. It was sent to Delhi for the Indian Railway Centenary celebration, but vanished immediately afterwards and is now considered lost.

In May 1854, the Bombay–Thane line was extended to Kalyan over the Thane viaducts (India's first railway bridges). Elsewhere in eastern India, the first East Indian Railway passenger train left Howrah (near Calcutta) to Hoogly (West Bengal), a distance of 39 km, on 15 August 1854. That same year, the GIPR opened its first railway workshops in Byculla, near Bombay. In 1855, the Bombay, Baroda & Central India Railway Company was created.

Southern India's first passenger train ran from Madras to Arcot, a distance of 97 km, on 1 July 1856. It was built and operated by the Madras Railway whose workshops opened in Perambur (near Madras) in that year. In 1858, the Eastern Bengal Railway was incorporated, with a view on linking India with Burma by rail. 1874 saw the creation of the South Indian Railway Company, through the merger of the Great South Indian and Carnatic State Railways.

The Indian railway system continued to grow right through the turn of the century and WWI, despite periods of civil unrest and widespread riots in all parts of the country. On 3 February 1925, the first electric passenger train in India (1,500 V DC) ran between Bombay's Victoria Terminus and Kurla. Electrification of the Bombay-Poona main line was achieved in 1929. The Indian Frontier Mail made its inaugural run between Bombay and Peshawar (in northern Pakistan, meaning "high fort") in 1928. The Grand Trunk Express began running between Peshawar and Mangalore, and the Punjab Limited served Bombay and Lahore. On 1 June 1930, the prestigious Deccan Queen officially entered service on the above-mentioned electrified route from Bombay to Poona.

A quick look at the post-independence era is provided to appreciate the changes made to the Indian railway system after 1947 and the end of the British Raj. In the wake of the new political reality and the division of the Empire into several new states, the national system was reorganized in 1951 into the new administrative regions of the Southern Railway and the Central and Western Railways of India. The Chief Commissariat of Railways was replaced with the Indian Railway Board. The Northern, Eastern and North Eastern Railway zones were created in April 1952. One novelty on Indian trains in the fifties was the introduction of fans and electric lights in all classes, with sleeping accommodations added to all long-haul trains. India's first fully air conditioned train was introduced between Howrah and Delhi in 1956.

Electrification could now proceed with full speed. In 1957, after successful trials in France, SNCF's proposed 25 kV AC system for India's railways was accepted. The Main Line Electrification Project was launched and the first scheduled train using 25 kV AC traction ran (on the Kharswan-Dangoaposi route) on 11 August 1960.

East Indian Railway 2-2-2 Nr. 21 "Express" (Kitson-Hewitson, Leeds 480 / 1856)

LONDON TO BOMBAY IN A WEEK: THE PROPOSED £21,000,000 RAILWAY.

DRAWN BY W. R. ROBINSON.

LINKING UP RUSSIA AND INDIA: THE SUGGESTED INTERNATIONAL LINE THROUGH PERSIA, CONNECTING THE RAILWAYS OF RUSSIA AND INDIA.

M. Zvegintseff, a member of the Duma, has stated that a number of Russians interested in financial and railway enterprise have decided that the time is ripe for the uniting of the lines of the European railway system with that of India. They propose to start from Baku, the southernmost station on the Russian system, and to take a direct line through Persia to Nushki, on the Anglo-Indian system. The length of line required to connect the Russian and Indian lines is 1600 miles, and it is said that the total expenditure called for would be £21,000,000. It is claimed that if the proposition be carried out, it will be possible to take passengers and mails from London to Bombay in eight days six hours: that is to say, at an average speed of twenty-eight miles an hour. A through ticket from London to Bombay would cost about £40.

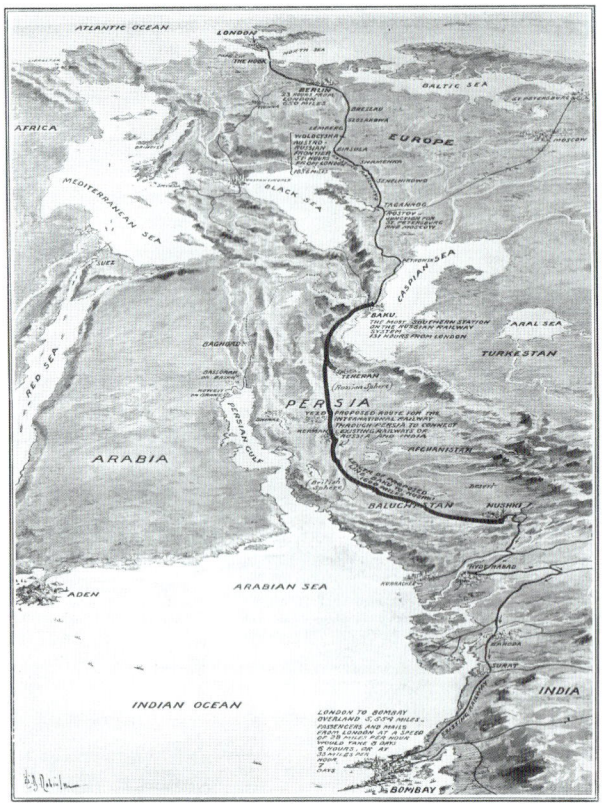

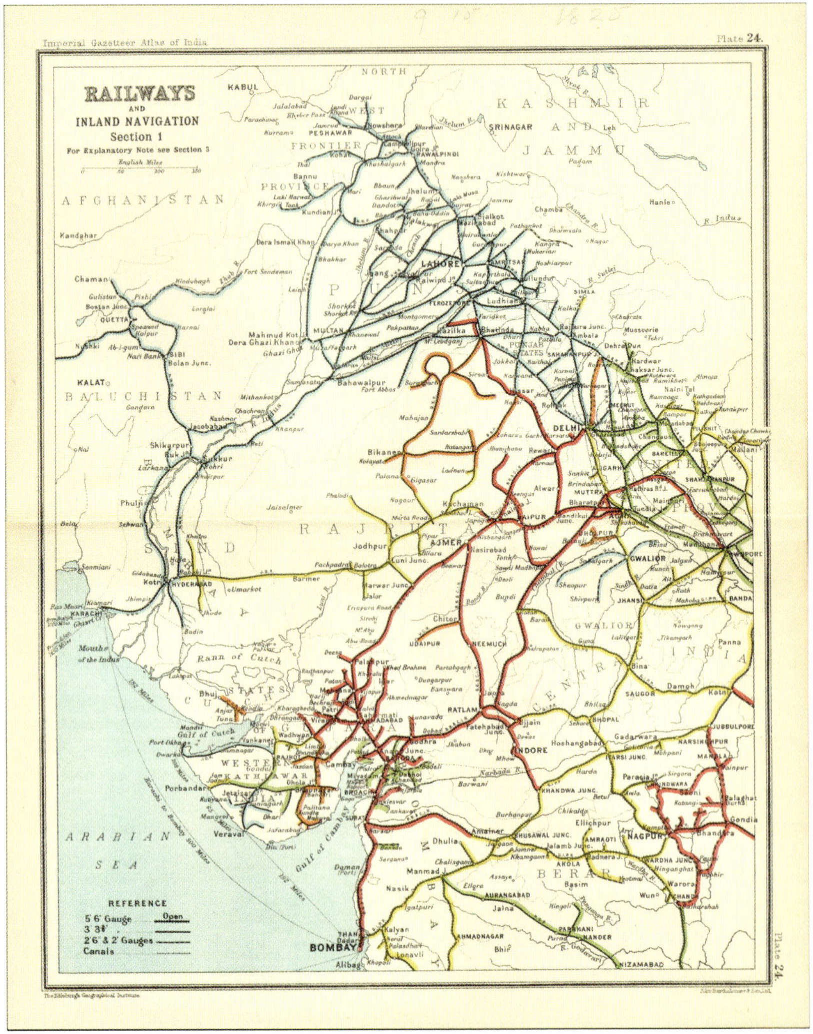

Far Left A map showing the proposed international London to Bombay railway, from The Illustrated London News, 26 November 1910.

Left, Right and Following Page India Railways - Railways & Inland Navigation Map (Imperial Gazetteer Atlas of India, 1931).

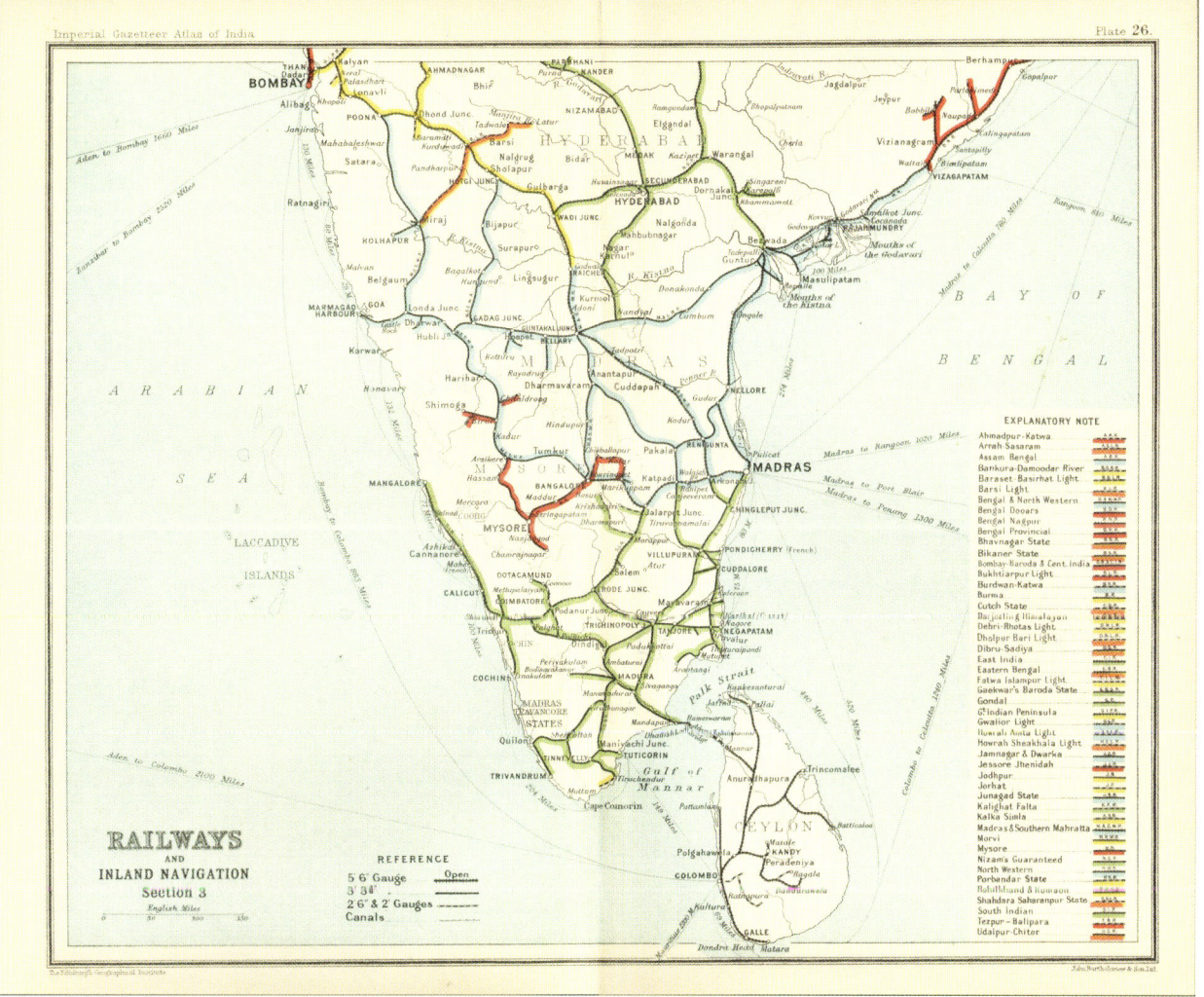

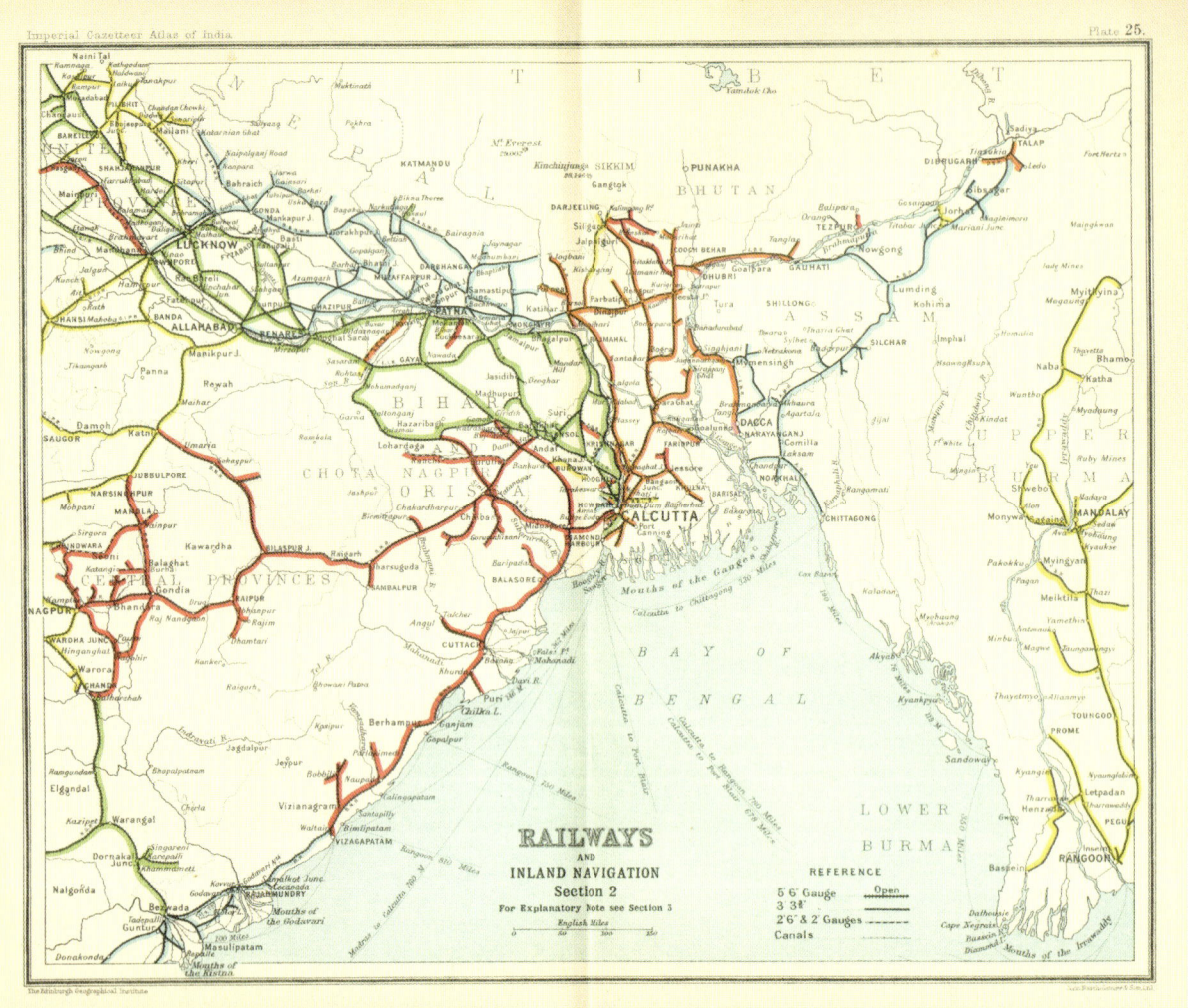

Growth and Expansion

"DREAMERS of action, impressed with the wonderful revolution created by the steam locomotive on the social and commercial life of Great Britain, decided to carry the railway to other parts of the British Empire" – so goes the story behind the construction of many new railway lines in the British colonies in Africa and Asia. Of these, no other colony was as promising as India, with its prosperous industries and profitable agriculture, but with primitive roads and inadequate means of transport. Early attempts were made to advance the development of railways in India but surprisingly, the British Governor-General, Lord Ellenborough, was against such a plan, calling it "all moonshine!" In the face of strong opposition from the East India Company, as little as 200 miles of planned track was only partly approved for construction by 1852, when the matter was brought before the new Governor, Lord Dalhousie. Appearing before him was John Chapman, a London businessman who was determined to build the first railway line in India. Chapman's attempt succeeded and in August 1845, he was in Bombay to investigate a route to Calcutta. His visit coincided with a railway mania in Britain and the previously negative attitude had happily given way to a new pro-railway policy.

Chapman's plan, however, depended heavily on the EIC's financial support, and was at first nearly rejected. His determination and persistence were rewarded when, on 01 August 1849, the decision was passed to accept his scheme and allocate a budget for the construction of the Great Indian Peninsula Railway's first line from Bombay to Kalyan. Amusingly, the EIC's approval was accompanied with a warning that spending money on offices and train stations was a waste of money and "a great error," continuing, "our special desire is that everything will be constructed as cheaply as possible, and with no unnecessary ornaments." This statement seems comical today, when compared with Bombay's iconic Victoria Terminus which is one of the grandest railway terminals in the world.

Chapman then set out to secure the services of the legendary railway pioneer, Robert Stephenson, who was persuaded to accept the appointment of consulting engineer to the new project right up to his death in 1859. It was a wise decision, since Bombay is an island and the new line was supposed to run through muddy wetlands on the way to mainland India. Stephenson had to overcome similar swamps when building the Liverpool and Manchester Railway in England and was an expert on the matter.

Work began on 08 February 1852 and the gauge chosen was 1,676 mm (broad gauge). That same day also saw the debut of the steam locomotive in India. This historic locomotive, the "Falkland" (0-4-0T, E. B. Wilson 1852), was actually used to carry ballast for the track. The British considered it as a way to let the unsophisticated natives get used to the "iron horse", in the hope that "this will reduce the risk of accidents which might otherwise happen upon the first running of the trains." Indeed, Falkland proved to be an object of such extreme curiosity and fascination that the natives flocked in their thousands to watch the little wonder running up and down the line, amazed to see the train moving as if by magic.

Meanwhile in Britain, the future of the Indian railways was placed in Lord Dalhousie's hands. Previously a member of the British Board of Trade, Dalhousie greatly believed in the railway's future and accordingly, supported the investment in a large-scale railway system in India. His report on this matter remains one of the most important documents ever written by a British statesman on Indian affairs and is considered to be the Indian railway system's Magna Carta.

Immediately following Lord Dalhousie's report, the Great Indian Peninsula Railway doubled its efforts to complete the long main line in the direction of Calcutta. Some 10,000 natives were employed, with the work moving forward with fantastic speed. The first section of the line, to Kalyan, was ready for opening on 04 April 1853, in only fourteen months. The problem of building a railway over Bombay's swamps was solved by repeating Robert Stephenson's proven method. Large sheets, made locally from mangrove trees, were placed on the mud, with a layer of stable soil above them to press the sheets down. This was repeated with more layers, until finally solid ground was created below the rails.

With the line open and trains running regularly, it was generally believed

Ceylon Government Railways - CGR Class D1 2-6-4ST Nr. 270 (Robert Stephenson Locomotive Works 3969 / 1928)

that Europeans will be the only passengers. India, so it was thought, was so full of religious prejudices that the natives will never ride the train. There may have been some truth in such a view, but the convenience of train travel had soon overtaken any conservative religious traditions. In reality, native Indians crowded into the trains to such an overwhelming extent that fourth class was proposed to carry the seemingly endless multitude of the poorest of passengers.

The GIPR line out of Bombay had now gotten as far as Kalyan Junction, where the trans-peninsula route was expected to run to the north-east, with another line to the south-east to Madras. Both lines had to overcome the formidable obstacle of the Western Ghats. The Ghat is a pass through a huge vertical mountain wall that reaches up to a height of 2,000 feet, posing a challenge of unprecedented proportions anywhere in India. Several options were considered, taking into account the steep inclines and the safety of the trains over this difficult section of the line. Again, Robert Stephenson was called in to help. Stephenson recommended a pass right through the mountains, at Thull, and that the construction of the line should advance with all available speed. Two passes, the Thull and Bhore Ghat Inclines, were finally approved and work began in January 1856 and in 1857, respectively. They remain an outstanding achievement of railway engineering to this day. Each incline included a reversing station, so that the locomotive could run around the train on the long way up to the next section.

The original Thull Ghat Incline was ten miles long, with a height difference of 972 feet. For five miles of the section, the locomotive had to climb a demanding grade of 1 in 37 with tight curves of a radius of 1,122 feet. Thirteen tunnels were built, the longest tunnel measuring 870 feet. Six large viaducts were also needed and of these, the Ehegaon Viaduct (750 feet long, completed in 1865) carries the track at 190 feet above the bottom of the gorge, and remains the highest in India. Safety was a prime concern on the Ghat section and although every possible measure was used to keep the trains under control, this was not always the case. On 26 January 1869, a descending train on the Bhore Ghat ran away despite the driver's desperate effort to slow it down to the legal speed of thirty km/h. The train rolled down the line into the reversing station at speed, going over the steep slope where it crashed down the hillside. Nineteen passengers and crew were killed, while another 42 were injured. The disaster was found to be due to slippery rails and the driver's fault of not using sand for better grip, excessive speed, and wrong use of the brakes. Following that tragedy, catch points were built on both Ghats in case of another runaway train.

On the crossing of the two Ghats, the main line to Calcutta could now continue from the top of the Thull Ghat Pass. At a point 276 miles out of Bombay, the line was divided due east to Nagpur (520 miles from Bombay) on the Central Route, where it connected with the eastern railway, continuing the route to Calcutta over a total of 1,300 miles from Bombay. Jubbulpore, 616 miles away from Bombay, was reached on 08 March 1870, linking with the East Indian Railway's Midland Route. A year later, in 1871, the railway reached Raichur Junction, where is joined the rest of the system to Madras and southern India. The opening of the 340 miles to Jubbulpore was the occasion of a great celebration, with a ceremony attended by H.R.H. the Duke of Edinburgh and the Viceroy of India.

The completion of the three main lines across the country led to an expansion of the system into local and rural communities, using a smaller gauge, with a view to cheaper construction costs. The first of these light railways was opened for traffic in March 1870 and thousands of miles of similar small lines were added in the following years.

By 1910, the Indian railway system became one of the largest in the world, with a total of 42,000 miles of multi-gauge track divided among 58 companies. Seven companies were officially designated as First Class Railways because their annual earnings were more than £300,000 (in 1910 values) and financially, exceeding anything ever anticipated when they were first created. As for the question of gauge, the North Western, East Indian, Great Indian Peninsula and Bengal Nagpur lines, with the main lines of the Madras and Southern Mahratta (MSMR) and the Bombay, Baroda and Central India (BBCIR) Railways, formed the main routes serving India's major ports, and were all broad gauge. The secondary railway systems of central and southern India, Burma and the State of Assam, were mostly meter gauge.

Above all, the system helped to unify the people of India by overcoming a long list of domestic problems. On top of the incredible size of the subcontinent, there was the climate which changed from the steaming heat

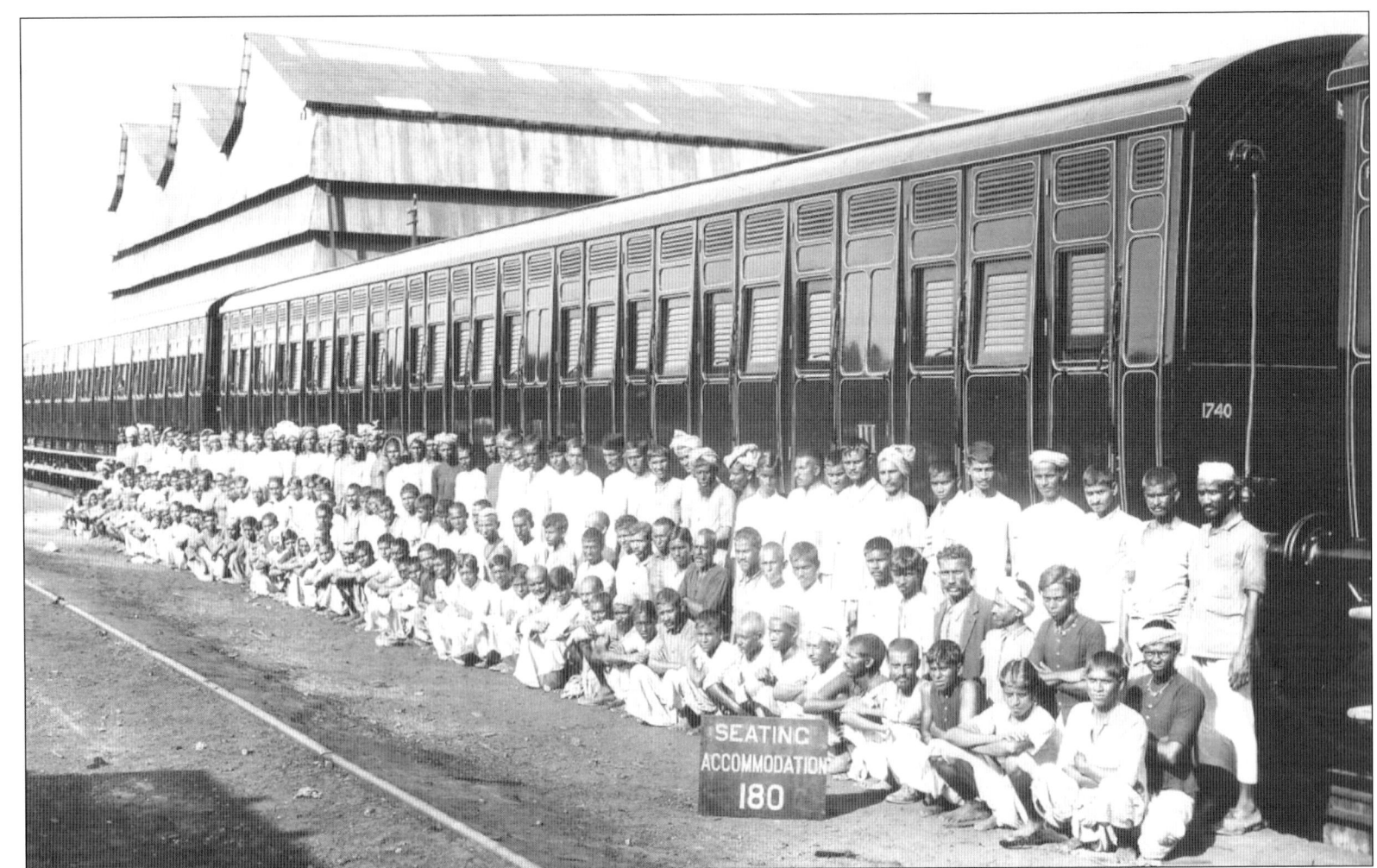
An Eastern Bengal Railway carriage poses for an official photograph

of the south to the freezing cold of the north. The journey from Bombay to Peshawar, for example, involved at first a voyage through tropical heat, then moving into arctic conditions in the North Western Frontier Province. The geographical difficulties varied from high mountains and dry deserts to tropical jungles and malaria swamps. Finally, there was the population of 350 million Indians, mostly living in poor agricultural communities, and speaking in a hundred different languages. Indeed, train travel in India was often a bizarre adventure for the inexperienced Western tourist on his first visit to the country, even though he had a choice of three classes. The first class was reserved for Europeans, the Indian aristocracy and senior officials. The second class was popular with the Indian middle class, and the poorest passengers had to join the mass of humanity in the 120 narrow wooden seats and no toilets or ventilation of the third class coach.

The 1920s were marked by a steady rise in the number of tourists and other visitors travelling to India, along with a gradual improvement in the living standards (the Indian railway system had by then reached a record length of 61,200 km). One notable aspect of this was the introduction of long-distance mail trains, which became necessary since India's main attractions are all hundreds of miles apart. The destinations selected for these deluxe trains were Bombay, Madras, Calcutta and Karachi, running all the long way to Delhi and the North Western Frontier. Bombay and Calcutta, being India's most important commercial centers, were provided with the Blue Train, India's equivalent of the Orient Express. It was a premium first class hotel-on-wheels especially equipped to carry passengers to the ocean-crossing mail steamers at Bombay in great comfort.

Two leading examples of these trains were the Bombay-Delhi Frontier Mail, operated jointly by the Bombay, Baroda and Central India and the North Western Railways, and the East Indian Railway's Punjab Mail (Calcutta-Delhi). Both trains covered a distance of 900 miles in 23 hours, including stops for locomotive changing, platform time and refueling. The Grand Trunk Express, India's longest direct railway route, departed from India's southern tip and proceeded due north through the rice fields of Madras and the cotton flatland of the Deccan Region into the jungles of Central India and Delhi, and onwards across Punjab to Peshawar, the gateway to the lands beyond the Himalaya mountains.

Romance and reality: the two faces of British India's railways

As with the rest of the British Empire, the Indian railway system was central to normal life in the Crown's leading colony. One obvious aspect of Britain's determination to remain in power in India for as long as it possibly could was an effort to constantly upgrade the system and the equipment that ran on it with modern locomotives and rolling stock, and by laying new lines everywhere. This policy remained in effect up to the 1930s, when new investments began to dry up in light of the strong nationalistic demands for Indian independence. In 1947, when Britain finally pulled out of India, that same system was left behind in an overall poor condition and with a fleet of outdated and worn out trains. Moreover, the demise of the British Raj also saw the end of the Prestigious Trains, which were the height of colonial-era luxury and were operated primarily, if not exclusively, for the benefit of the ruling white class.

India's prestigious trains were conceived to provide their passengers with the finest level of service imaginable. Made of only First and Second Class, they were the elite trains in India, and punctual to the dot. Their legacy and impression on India's heritage under the British continue to this day. The modern successor of the Frontier Mail, now renamed The Golden Temple Mail (Mumbai – New Delhi – Amritsar), is the fastest train on the route. Other grand trains were the Mangalore – Peshawar Express, the Indian Imperial Mail, the Flying and Boat Mail, the Deccan Queen, and the Taj Express.

The service standards on these trains were easily some of the best in the world. In this case, this meant the comfort of plush seats in handsome coaches that were divided into individual suites and whose interiors included carpeting, electric lights and fans, large clean beds, private showers, servants and a choice of beverages. Some trains even had an air-conditioning system using a big block of ice that was lowered into a slot in the floor or the roof. Unlike modern trains, however, the first class carriages did not have any corridors. Each single suite was actually a separate room with its own side doors that opened right to the platform.

Equally comfortable, though less luxurious, was the second class coach with its cushioned seats. It was the preferred mode of transport for most Europeans. The third class coach consisted of simple wooden benches,

Madras and Southern Mahratta Railway - 4-6-2 steam locomotive Nr. 900 "New York" (Baldwin Locomotive Works 57738 / 1924). This was one of a pair delivered in that year.

without any lights, fans or toilets, and was routinely full to capacity with Indians. The fourth class coach was an empty boxcar with a few windows and no seats at all, and crammed with the poorest passengers in horrendous conditions. The crucial majority of the native Indian population could barely afford, and was accordingly restricted, to travel only by third or fourth class while non-Indian passengers enjoyed the luxury of the first and second class. The conditions in the fourth class were appalling enough that it was finally abolished and a new class named "intermediate" or "inter" was introduced between the second and third classes, with a few rows of seats. It was not until 1955 that third class was formally cancelled in India.

Glorious trains aside, there were other, more down-to-earth trains throughout the Indian railway system, connecting the cities of India with the countryside. And where the famous express trains had automatic priority over any other train, ordinary trains were slow and time-consuming because most lines were single track, holding up the trains with an inevitably long delay. Also, some first class mail trains needed a long platform time so that their passengers could dine at the station restaurant. For the many millions of Indians who weren't fortunate enough to ride on a mail train, it was an all but romantic experience. The striking difference between the dreamlike service on any first class mail train and the often traumatic ride inside a third class coach wasn't lost even on Gandhi, the father and symbol of India's struggle for independence, who travelled extensively through India starting in 1920. As an important political leader, he had the right to travel in second class, but insisted on boarding the overcrowded third class coach, where he had to squeeze in with his countrymen, in protest against the British treatment of native Indian passengers.

Indeed, no other element in the controversial history of the British Raj demonstrates the profound difference between the British colonial rulers and their governed native Indians as the story of the railways of India up to 1947. However glamorous and romantic they might have been, the fact is that the railways of British India thrived above all on a good deal of show and appearance. They were made to serve firstly the high ranking British administration of India, then the centers of commerce and industry, and only then the native population, if at all. It was a tragic mistake that cost the British their biggest colony, and with a shocking loss of life.

Post-Independence: The railways in the wake of the British Raj

India received its independence from Britain in 1947, officially ending the European colonial period in the Asian subcontinent. The new reality of self-rule was also a turning point for the railways of that country, whose giant system was in a condition that was far from perfect as a result of the war effort and the gradual decline of new investments in infrastructure ever since the 1930s.

Upon the British administration's departure, India's railways were arranged not as one single company, but as a patchwork of some fifty separate systems with little government control and no standardization of rolling stock and equipment. Many of the steam locomotives were shipped overseas during WWII, to help with the British war effort in the Middle East, and the ones that remained behind were cannibalized and in need of repair and overhaul. There were only a few new orders for rolling stock, in part also due to the war's impact on Britain's own economy and the temporary difficulty of manufacturing new locomotives, since most British factories were converted to building planes and tanks. The supply of new equipment for the railways both at home and in the colonies abroad, had to wait until production could be resumed, but only after peace was restored in Europe and the British industry was back on its feet after six years of war with Hitler's Germany.

One immediate outcome of India's independence was the carving up of the Raj into several new states outside India's borders, which now had to be redrawn to reflect the desires of the hostile Hindu and Muslim communities that were previously living under one central British rule. The partition of India was essentially religiously-motivated, so that followers of each specific faith were given a piece of the total territory. For the railways of the former Raj, this posed yet another challenge. Whole sections of the Indian system were now across the border and out of reach. The railway companies themselves were already transferred from British to Indian hands and, after a transition period, the latter were expected to assume responsibility over the country's national railway system, while taking into account the complicated political relationships with the newly-created neighboring countries of Pakistan, Bangladesh, Burma and Sri Lanka (formerly Ceylon). It was not an easy task. The Assam Bengal Railway

Bengal Nagpur Railway steam locomotive Nr. 155 taking water. Note the puppy standing on the locomotive's buffer beam. BNR steam locomotive Nr. 155 was delivered new to India in 1900 (BNR Nrs. 144-158 / SS 4575-89).

(ABR) remained with East Pakistan (now Bangladesh), along with India's entire Northeastern region which was cut off from the rest of the country. Only 388 km of India's entire route length was electrified, with the Bombay–Poona main line being the only electric route in the country. Most of the track was meter and broad gauge. The locomotive fleet was a mix of the old and the new, with five gauges (broad, standard, meter, narrow and industrial) and a handful of diesel units. In 1950, there were 8,120 steam, 72 electric (mostly suburban EMUs) and seventeen diesel locomotives in India. Pre-1947, the total track mileage in India was around 83,000 km. That impressive number was now reduced by 25,000 km, which ended up mostly in Pakistan. Routes, timetables, schedules and fares all had to be reformed to fit the needs of the Indian government, whose plans and interests were different from those of the former British rulers. To aggravate matters, the massive disturbances around the partition plan grew into violent riots. Normal operations were suspended indefinitely and instead, the railways began moving hundreds of thousands of refugees both in and outside India. In the midst of anarchy and massacre, the railways also had to regroup on each side of the border. Employees, property, equipment and everything else had to be divided between the new Asian states. When the dust finally settled down and the independence-induced conflict was over, India was, for the first time in that country's history, ready and willing to rebuild the railway system without any foreign interference. The British Raj was over.

PROGRAMME OF EVENTS AT JAMRUD.

7·45 a.m.	Down Country Special arrives.
9·10 a.m.	Local Guests' Special from Peshawar arrives.
9·30 a.m.	Guests are requested to be in their seats.
9·50 a.m.	His Excellency the Commander-in-Chief and Guests of Government House, Peshawar, arrive by motor car.
10·0 a.m.	The Hon'ble Sir Charles Innes, K.C.S.I., C.I.E., arrives, accompanied by the Chief Commissioner, N.-W. F. Province.
	Presentation of Railway Officers.
10·5 a.m.	Address by the Chief Commissioner of Railways.
	Reply by the Hon'ble Sir Charles Innes, K.C.S.I., C.I.E.
	<u>*The Message from His Excellency the Viceroy is read.*</u>
	(*Guests are requested to stand while Sir Charles Innes reads the message from His Excellency the Viceroy.*)
	The Hon'ble Sir Charles Innes, K.C.S.I., C.I.E., pulls the lever and releases the gates which slowly open.

Above Programme of the official opening of the Khyber Pass Railway on November 2nd, 1925 at Jamrud.

Left An Indian State Railways poster showing the Khyber Pass with three native Indians and a steam locomotive and train emerging from a tunnel.

Broad gauge, oil fired steam locomotive, class HGS 2-8-0 2216 (Kitson, Leeds 5104 / 1914), with 2264 at the rear, perform a runpast for photographers with a charter train at Shahgai, on the Khyber Pass, 23 December 1993, on the way back to Jamrud, near Peshawar. Local tribesmen are asserting their right to free travel on the trains, a condition of the railway being built through their land. Nr. 2216 was originally North Western Railway Nr. 1766, then became Pakistan Railways 2216 in 1947.
© Nigel Tout

Indian Government Railways Class HPS 4-6-0 steam locomotives 7773-6 at Birkenhead Docks (UK), October 1949 (Vulcan Foundry 5750-5833 / 1949)

An official photo of several new metre gauge Class A 4-6-0 steam locomotives (Works Nos 2488 to 2493) for the Gaekwar's Baroda State Railway in India under construction at Bagnall's in Stafford in 1933.

Bengal Nagpur Railway (BNR) de Glehn 4-4-2 steam locomotive Nr. 2 (North British Locomotive Works 17818 / 1908)

Great Indian Peninsula Railway 4-6-0 steam locomotive Nr. 389 with the Royal Mail train outside Bombay train station.
Thirteen of these locomotives were delivered to the GIPR by Vulcan Foundry in 1912 (VF 2805-17).

Central Railway of India (ex-Barsi Light Railway) Class F 2-8-2 steam locomotive Nr. 720 (Nasmyth, Wilson Locomotive Works 1575 / 1929).

North Western Railway of Pakistan - Lahore train station on a vintage postcard.

Great Indian Peninsula Railway - GIPR Class WCG1 electric locomotive "Sir Leslie Wilson" (SLM Winterthur 3197 / 1928) and passenger train.

Class WDM1 diesel locomotive Nr. 17099 (Alco 83136 / 1958) at Kharagpur Shed on 17 February 1978.

Above Central Railway of India (ex-GIPR) Class WCP/2 electric locomotive Nr. 20024 "Sir Roger Lumley" (SLM Winterthur 3643 / 1938). The WCP/1 were the first electric locomotives to run in India. They were used for passenger operations on the 1500 V dc Bombay-Poona route. They heralded the arrival of high speed train travel in India, as they used to cover the 192 km steeply graded Bombay-Poona run with the 7-car Deccan Queen in 2 hr. 45 min. in the 1930s.

Left A Great Indian Peninsula Railway poster advertising the special Poona Races deluxe train, in the charge of Scottish-built 4-6-0 steam locomotive Nr. 211 (NBL Glasgow, 1903). This was the fastest seasonal service between Mumbai (then Bombay) and Pune (then Poona) prior to electrification and before the arrival of The Deccan Queen, covering the 192 km distance in under four hours with three locomotive changes and the reversal at Bhore Ghat. The next fastest regular train, the Poona Mail, used to take up to six hours to cover the same distance.

A sepia photo of East Indian Railway steam locomotive Nr. 213, built by Neilson of Glasgow in 1893. It was one out of 25 such locomotives delivered to India within the same year, with the EIR road Nrs. 205-229 (Neilson 4546-4570). Additional Class A locos arrived also from Dübs and Co., in 1893 and again in 1899.

A May 1919 photo of British troops returning from the riots at Bombay, in Great Indian Peninsula Railway bogie coach Nr. 4749.

First Class coaches of the standard pattern adopted on the North Western Railway of India and on the Nowshera Durgai Railway, the latter being a narrow gauge railway (1903).

Hubli steam locomotive workshops, circa 1900. The workshop was inaugurated in 1885, serving the Southern Mahratta railway. In 1908, it became part of the Madras and Southern Mahratta Railway (MSMR). Post-independence, it belonged initially to the Southern Railway and was then transferred to the South Central Railway in 1966, before ending up with the South Western Railway of India. The depot handled YG and YP steam locomotives in later years.

Official photo showing the Interior of the Royal Train carrying the Prince of Wales and his staff during their visit to India

Malakwal Junction on the Pakistan Railways network sees locomotives Nrs. 3078 (Beyer Peacock 4612 / 1904) & 2964 (Vulcan Foundry 2771 / 1911)

Indian Railways Class WP steam locomotive Nr. 7599 (Canadian Locomotive Company, 1955) at Erode in 1977.

Madras Egmore train station in November 1982. © Stephen Owens

A heavy goods train on the Thull Ghaut incline near Kasara, on the Great Indian Peninsula Railway's main line to Calcutta from Bombay via Jubbulpore, being hauled by a 2-10-0 four-cylinder oil burning locomotive assisted by an eight-coupled Ghaut tank locomotive (Y3 type) in the centre of the train, and another engine of the same class at the rear.

India's hill railways

None of India's many historical attractions is as rewarding as the so-called Hill Railways, affectionately known as "India's toy trains." These amazing mountain lines were built long before WWI, so that British government officials could escape from the infernal heat of the Indian summer to the cool air of the highlands. The mountain trains continue to run to this day, to the immense joy and delight of both regular travelers and visitors alike. A train ride on a hill railway in India is a unique experience. The steep climb to the mountaintop is breathtaking. The line crosses a series of bridges and tunnels, set in the most beautiful landscape imaginable, with incredibly tight twists and turns as the train proceeds uphill to the summit station. Steam locomotives are still in operation on some of these fascinating lines, and a closer look at their history is therefore in order.

India's hill railways are widely scattered across the land, whose northern border runs along the Himalaya mountain range for thousands of miles. In southern India rises the Nilgiri, and the previously-mentioned Ghats (meaning "a mountain pass" or "a route through hills") overlook the country's western coastline. These natural obstacles, although difficult to cross, provide a welcomed relief from the unforgiving Indian tropical climate, and the British wasted no time in taking advantage of the tall hills, far above the blistering heat of the valleys below. Also, much of India's trade travels over the mountains to the main ports. Hence the need for railways to and through the mountains.

As was common with the Indian railway system, the hill lines too were built to four gauges – broad (1,676 mm or 5 ft 6 in), one meter, narrow (762 mm or 2 ft 6 in) , and the tiny gauge of 600 mm (two feet). Listed below are the four best known lines:

South Indian Railway – Nilgiri Mountain Railway (NMR 46 km, one metre gauge)

The Nilgiri line is both India's only meter gauge and Abt rack and pinion hill railway. Swiss (SLM Winterthur) 0-8-2T steam locomotives are used with a few small diesels. Coming from the downhill station, the rack section leads into Coonoor station (used as location in Sir David Lean's 1984 Oscar-winning movie A Passage to India). Ootacamund, once the summer headquarters of the Government of Madras, is reached right beyond the line's summit, which is 7,228 feet above sea level. This is one of the most attractive hill stations in India, with a park of English wild flowers. The Nilgiri Mountain Railway was declared a UNESCO World Heritage Site in July 2005.

NMR 2-4-0T rack locomotive (one of Beyer Peacock 3875-7, 3925 / 1897) and train on Kullar Bridge. Illustration from The Engineer, 31 March 1899.

North Western Railway – Kangra Valley Railway & Kalka Shimla Railway (KVR 163 km & KSR 96 km, 762 mm gauge)

Afoot the Himalaya lies the Kangra Valley, whose hill railway covers a distance of 163 km between Pathankot and Joginder Nagar in a huge nature reserve and ancient Hindu shrines. The highest point on this line is at 1,291 m (4,236 feet).

The "Kangra Toy Train" was inaugurated in 1929, and is today operated by the Northern Railway of India. It is made of no fewer than 971 bridges and two tunnels. Locally-built diesels are used regularly, but at the time of writing an effort is made to reintroduce steam trains on the KVR.

The Kalka Shimla Railway runs between Kalka Junction and the Indian-alpine holiday town of Shimla. The KSR reaches an altitude of 2,076 m (6,811 feet) in the Himalaya Mountains. Shimla became the summer government center of British India as early as 1864 and the line was built in 1898, taking four years to reach the summit station.

The Kalka Shimla Railway was added to the UNESCO World Heritage List in 2008.

Commercial postcard of the Kalka Shimla Railway.

A Northern Railway of India 2' 6" gauge K Class 2-6-2 tank locomotive, one of a class built by North British between 1904 and 1910, heads a freight train on the spectacular Kalka – Simla line in 1970. This type was supplied as saturated locos to the original operating company by the North British Locomotive Company between 1904 and 1910. Many were later fitted with superheaters and reclassified as KC.

Darjeeling Himalayan Railway (DHR 88 km, 610 mm gauge)

The most famous of all of India's hill lines, The Darjeeling Himalayan Railway is the lifeline of the Darjeeling (West Bengal) tea-growing district. The line's highest elevation is at Ghoom station (2,300 m / 7,500 feet). It is in fact a branch line off the main line to Calcutta. The journey to Darjeeling originally required the use of horse-drawn carts on a dirt road. A transportation committee was appointed to review the situation and a recommendation was issued to build a narrow gauge railway. It was a brilliant decision and a wise business move. Work began in 1879 and was completed in July 1881. By 1910, the DHR carried an impressive annual total of 174,000 passengers and 47,000 tons of freight, most of it bags of premium Darjeeling tea. 34 0-4-0ST British and American steam locomotives were once needed to meet the line's traffic demands, but have since then been replaced with six diesels. A few of the steam locomotives are kept for steam specials and a single 0-4-0+0-4-0 Garratt (Beyer Peacock, 1910) remained in service until 1954.

The DHR was India's first mountain railway to enter the UNESCO World Heritage List in 1999.

DHR 0-4-0ST Nr. 777 (Sharp Stewart & Co, Atlas Works, Manchester 3517 / 1889)

DHR Class B 0-4-0ST steam locomotive Nr. 795 (Tindharia Workshops, 1919)

Matheran Hill Railway (Western Ghats Region) (21 km, 610 mm gauge)

The Matheran Hill Railway is a 21 km line between Neral and Matheran, in the Western Ghats area. The route was first designed in 1900 and completed in 1907, remaining an engineering marvel to this day. The line consists of several horseshoe embankments and a tunnel that is romantically known as "One Kiss Tunnel" (so called because it is long enough to send a kiss to the last coach). The broad gauge line to Bombay runs near the Matheran Hill Railway, and the two lines cross each other twice.

The MHR owned four 0-6-0T "Klien Lindner" type Orenstein & Koppel locomotives, built in 1905-07. A fifth locomotive arrived from Baldwin of Philadelphia in 1917. They are said to have run until 1982, when they were replaced by diesels. MHR Nr. 3 (O & K 2343 / 1907) was sold to the South Tynedale Heritage Railway in northern Britain and is awaiting a full restoration there.

Other steep sections include the spectacular (broad gauge) Khyber and Bolan Pass Railways, once in the northern Raj and today in Pakistan. The Great Indian Peninsula Railway's route from Bombay to mainland India, which is a good example of an Indian mainline hill railway through the Thull and Bhore Ghats, was converted from steam to electric traction in 1930. It was worked with two types of electric locomotive, 4-6-2 weighing 102 tons with six motors giving an output of 2,160 HP for passenger traffic and a heavier jackshaft-type 0-6-0 + 0-6-0 (2,600 HP) that often ran in pairs for hauling a combined weight of one thousand tons up and 1,600 tons downhill. The Bhore Ghat incline reaches a top altitude of 1,800 feet as the line climbs out of Bombay with 25 tunnels and eight long viaducts, forming the route of the "Deccan Queen" – India's then-fastest daily express train which covered the distance of 118 miles to Poona in only 175 minutes.

In British India's wild and rugged North Western Frontier (since 1947 in Pakistan), the Bolan Pass (broad gauge) line climbs up the vast and arid mountains to a fantastic level of 5,858 feet. Originally built as a meter gauge military railway, it carried troop trains literally to the edge of the British Empire at Quetta (altitude 5,499 feet) and through the Khojak Tunnel to Chaman, on the border with Afghanistan. Garratt locomotives were standard equipment on the Bolan Pass, along with the standard 4-8-0s, and both locomotives had to perform under freezing conditions in the winter and in temperatures as high as fifty degrees in the summer. Contrary to the area's desert-like appearance, fruit traffic from Kandahar to all parts of India was heavy throughout most of the year.

This commercial postcard shows MHR Nr. 2 (Orenstein & Koppel 2342 / 1907) and train

British India's steam and electric locomotives

Given its awe-inspiring size, the variety of gauge, the multitude of railway companies and the long period under British rule, it is understandably impossible to refer in detail to every single steam locomotive that ever ran in the Raj before (and indeed after) 1947. An estimated total of 30,000 locomotives were delivered to British India's rapidly growing railway system over the decades, with the majority coming from the workshops in Glasgow (North British), Manchester (Beyer Peacock), Newcastle (Robert Stephenson), Leeds (Kitson), Stafford (Bagnall) and above all, from Newton-le-Willows (Vulcan Foundry). They ranged from the tiny 0-4-0s of the Darjeeling Railway to Bengal's enormous broad gauge Garratts, with a "middle class" made of the usual freight and passenger locomotives. More steam locomotives arrived from Germany and America, although in minor numbers when compared with the ones ordered from Britain. Post-1947, new large orders were placed in America, Austria, Germany, Japan and Canada, and in 1958, even with Fablok of Chrzanów for thirty bullet-shaped Class WP Pacifics.

It could be argued with certainty that at the beginning of the twentieth century, no other railway system on earth relied on more different locomotive types than that of India. A Locomotive Standardization Committee was appointed in 1903 to address the problem. The solution found was to create a catalogue of several official designs, and let the railways choose the ones that fit them best. The committee specified a 4-4-0 locomotive for passenger and 0-6-0 for freight (both inside cylinder) with Belpaire firebox. An alternative, larger boiler was added to the catalogue in 1910 to deal with steep lines, requiring more power and a higher axle load. Further designs appeared in 1906 – 4-6-0 and 4-4-2 for mail trains, 2-8-0 and 2-8-2T for heavy freight traffic and a passenger 2-6-4. These standard types were known as BESA (British Engineering Standards Association) locomotives and were built in large numbers, since 1912 also with superheating.

A massive upsurge in post-WWI traffic resulted in a need for stronger locomotives. A second Locomotive Standards Committee was set up in 1924 to update and modernize the BESA designs and these came to be known as the Indian Railway Standards (IRS) locomotives.

Indian locomotive classes are designated using a prefix of one to three Latin letters. Thus, the Letters X and W denote a broad gauge locomotive. WP, for example, is a broad gauge express locomotive. Z and Q stand for narrow gauge. Other letters describe size, speed, power output, gauge, purpose (passenger or freight) and sometimes even the country of origin.

Electric trains first appeared in India in Bombay, where the local steam trains were gradually replaced with a network of suburban EMUs to improve efficiency and capacity. A similar need arose with the Bombay, Baroda & Central India Railway, whose route came down to one double line carrying both long-haul and local traffic into the city. In cooperation with the Great Indian Peninsula Railway, a decision was made to install an electric local service, capable of running on a five minute basis. The rolling stock was ordered from Cammell Laird in England and sent to India ready to run. The electrification of the suburban sections of the two railways was completed in 1928. Immediately afterwards the Great Indian Peninsula Railway decided to electrify its main line from Bombay to Poona, at that time one of the longest main line electrification projects in the world. The first all-electric train of that route began running on 01 June 1930 under the title "Deccan Queen."

Eastern Bengal Railway 4-6-2 Nr. 443 "Lord Dalhousie" (Armstrong Whitworth 1058 / 1930).

Bengal Nagpur Railway (BNR) K class de Glehn compound 4-4-2 Nr. 2.
Fifteen of these 4-4-2s were built between 1907 and 1914 by the North British Locomotive Works.

Madras & Southern Mahratta Railway 0-6-6-0 (North British Locomotive Works, 1910). Three of these Mallet locomotives were originally ordered by the West of India Portuguese Railway in 1910. They became MSMR 315-317 and carried the NBL works numbers 19325-19327.

Eastern Bengal State Railway class P 4-6-2 Nr. 147 (Robert Stephenson & Co. 3531 / 1913).

No. 55.

THE VULCAN LOCOMOTIVE WORKS.
"E F" CLASS
ELECTRIC FREIGHT LOCOMOTIVE
SUPPLIED BY MESSRS. METROPOLITAN-VICKERS ELECTRICAL CO. LTD.
— FOR —
THE GREAT INDIAN PENINSULA RAILWAY
MECHANICAL PARTS SUPPLIED BY VULCAN FOUNDRY LTD.

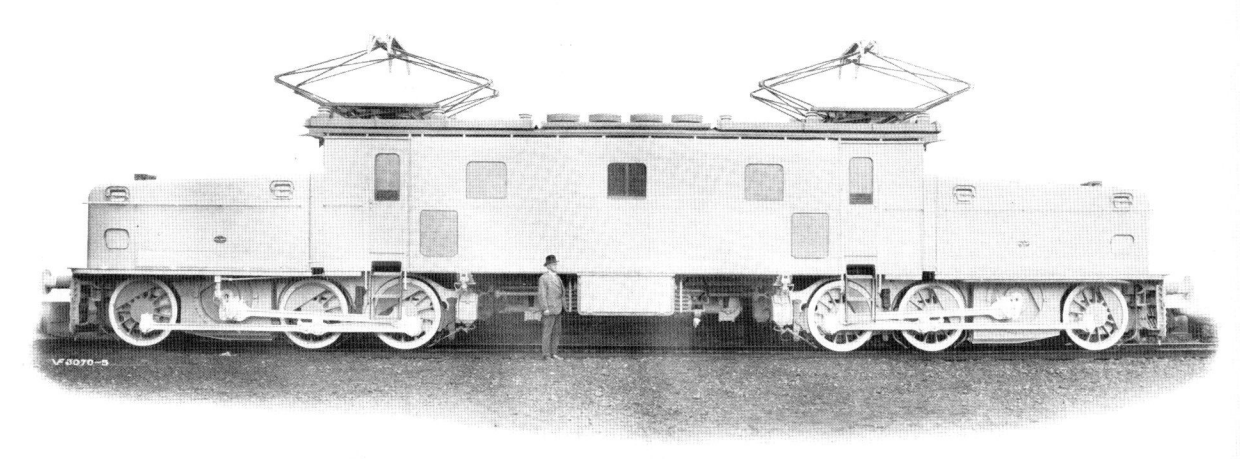

0-6-0 + 0-6-0 TYPE.   GENERAL DIMENSIONS.   **GAUGE 5 ft. 6 ins.**

WHEELS.
Diameter on Tread .... 4 ft. 9 ins.
Do. of Centre .... 3 ft. 6 ins.
Journals .... 8½ ins. × 11 ins.

WHEELBASE.
Truck Wheelbase .... 15 ft. 1 in.
Total Engine Wheelbase .... 54 ft. 11 in.
Total Length over Buffers .... 66 ft. 1 in.

BRAKE.
Air Brake Equipment on Loco.
Vacuum Brake Equipment for Train Working.

CHARACTERISTICS.
Direct Current Motors .... 4 Motors.
Overhead Line Pressure .... 1,500 Volts.
Capacity per Motor .... 650 H.P.
Total Capacity per Loco .... 2,600 H.P.

TRACTIVE EFFORT.
Maximum 125% coeff.1 .... 67,200 lbs.
Hourly Rating of 18 m.p.h. .... 56,000 lbs.
Continuous Rating of 20.5 m.p.h. .... 40,000 lbs.

SPEEDS.
Normal Service .... 35 m.p.h.
Safe Maximum .... 45 m.p.h.
Gear Ratio .... 1/4·13.

WEIGHT.
Maximum per Axle .... 20½ tons.
Total Mechanical Parts .... 72½ tons.
Total Electrical Parts .... 50½ tons.
Total Locomotive .... 123 tons.

SERVICE.
Goods.

Postal Address: NEWTON-LE-WILLOWS, LANCS., England.

Festival of Britain 1951 - Indian Government Railways Class WG (broad gauge) 2-8-2 steam locomotive Nr. 8350 (North British Locomotive Co, Glasgow - NBL 26464 / 1950).

Indian Government Railways 2-8-2 steam locomotive Nr. 8324 at George Square in Glasgow in 1950.
It was built by the North British Locomotive Company under the NBL works Nr. 26438 and entered service in India as class WG.

Great Indian Peninsula Railway - GIPR electric locomotive Nr. 4004 (SLM Winterthur & Metropolitan Vickers 3372 / 1929) and the Deccan Queen passenger train. This train took passengers between Poona (Pune) and Bombay (Mumbai), a distance of 118 miles. The line was electrified in 1929 to provide a more efficient service.

DECCAN QUEEN.

Indian Railways Class YP 4-6-2 steam locomotive Nr. 2343 (Telco 1957) and passenger train at Bangalore City station in 1977.

Six 2-8-2 steam locos (class YD 15-20) for the South Indian Railway (AEG Borsig 4577-4582 / 1931) being loaded for shipment to India.